To Johnny with love —T. R.

The editors would like to thank
BARBARA KIEFER, Ph.D., Associate Professor of Reading and Literature,
Teachers College, Columbia University, and
JIM BREHENY, Curator of Education for the Wildlife Conservation Society
at the Bronx Zoo, for their assistance in the preparation of this book.

Grolier Books is a division of Grolier Enterprises, Inc.

Library of Congress Cataloging-in-Publication Data
Rabe, Tish.
Is a camel a mammal? / by Tish Rabe.   p.   cm. —
(The Cat in the Hat's learning library)
SUMMARY: Dr. Seuss's Cat in the Hat introduces Sally and Dick to a variety
of mammals, from the fruit-eating bat to the smart chimpanzee.
ISBN 0-679-87302-3 (trade). — ISBN 0-679-97302-8 (lib. bdg.)
1. Mammals—Juvenile literature. [1. Mammals.] I. Title. II. Series.
QL706.2.R33   1998   599—dc21   97-52316

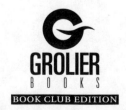

GROLIER
B O O K S
BOOK CLUB EDITION

IS A CAMEL A MAMMAL?

by Tish Rabe

illustrated by Jim Durk

The Cat in the Hat's Learning Library™

Random House New York

I'm the Cat in the Hat
and I'm writing a book.
It's all about mammals.
Come on, take a look!
From the fruit-eating bat
to the smart chimpanzee,
from the moles in their holes
to the seals in the sea.
From raccoons to baboons,
I will show them to you.
Your mother will not
mind at all if I do.

All mammals breathe air
and are warm to the touch.
Mammals grow hair.
Some a lot.
Some not much.
Their hair can be soft
like the fur on a kitten
or the wool from a lamb
you knit into a mitten.

Their hair can be hard
like this small hedgehog's spines
or the dangerous quills
on these two porcupines.

Mammals live on cold mountains

and hot, burning sand,

down deep in the oceans
or out on dry land.

They can hop, jump, and swim
or glide high on the breeze.

They can walk, run, and climb
or swing up in the trees.
They are full of surprises—
of that I've no doubt.
Is a camel a mammal?
Read on and find out.

What's the world's smallest mammal?
I've brought one for you.

14

It weighs less than a dime.
It's this cute...

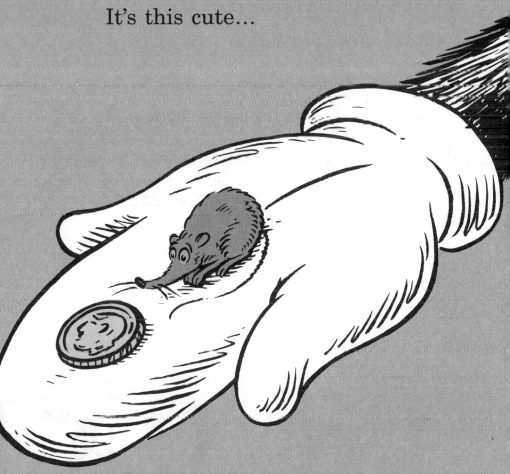

...pygmy shrew!

What's the world's largest mammal?
(I knew you would ask.)
You can figure it out
if you're up to the task.
Find some elephants,
each weighing twelve thousand pounds.
(Weighing elephants is just as
hard as it sounds!)

When you've got twenty-seven
stacked up on a scale,
you'll come close to the weight
of a single...

...blue whale!

This stupendulous mammal
lives under the sea,
and its baby, when born,
weighs two tons more than me!
Here's a fact about whales
that I learned from the Sneetches:
When one jumps out of water,
we say that it breaches!

And speaking of babies...
A hippopotamus baby
(a son or a daughter)
must swim right away
'cause it's born underwater.

And these bobcat kittens
have soft, furry paws—
but hidden inside them
are very sharp claws.

Baby bats are called batlings,
and bat moms, I hear,
give birth to just one little
batling each year.

When a mom armadillo
has babies, you'll find
she has four. They're all boys
or all girls—just one kind.

Each baby opossum's
the size of a bee!
Eighteen can fit into
a teaspoon, you see.

Kangaroos,
bandicoots,
and wallabies
have pouches to carry
their babies with ease.

Mammals come in all colors
and this helps protect them.
They're designed so their enemies
cannot detect them.
This snowshoe hare will
turn white when it snows,
from the tips of its ears
to its little pink nose.

But in spring when the snow melts,
its fur turns to brown.
It can hide then because
it blends in with the ground.

Skunks have black-and-white fur
that warns "Stop! Stay away!"
But if someone keeps trying
to get them to play,
they will stamp, then let loose
with a foul-smelling spray.
(Skunks tend to lose lots
of fun playmates that way!)

The polar bear, walrus,
sea lion, and otter
spend most of their time
in their home in the water.

A mother bear snuggles
right down in her cave
with her two little bear cubs
(who both are named Dave).
They sleep through each winter.
It's spring when they wake.
It's called hibernation,
this sleep that they take.

A giraffe, cow, or bison
has horns on its head.
Caribou, moose, and reindeer
have antlers instead.

Horns stay on forever,
but antlers, I hear,
fall off just like Thidwick's,
the same time each year.

Some mammals eat birds, reptiles,
insects, and fish,
and some prefer plants
as their favorite dish.
Pandas eat mostly
a grass called bamboo.
Koalas have only
one leaf they will chew.
Tigers and wolves can go
days without food,
but it tends to put them
in an unfriendly mood.

Anteaters never can
find time to play.
They have to eat thousands
of ants every day.

You may think that cheese
is what mice like to eat,
but they really like seeds
such as corn, oats, and wheat.

Carnivores love juicy meat.

Herbivores like plants to eat.

Omnivores, we do recall,

like meat and plants—

they eat it all!

Now here is the question
I want to ask you.
Is a camel a mammal?
You're right!
It is true.
They're the "ships of the desert."
They're called that, I know,
because camels take people
where they want to go—
across hot desert sands
or through cold, icy snow.
With its four padded feet,
it can walk without sinking
and go on for days—
even weeks—without drinking.

Long, heavy eyelashes!
Nostrils that close!
Keep the sand out
of its eyes and its nose!

37

My book about mammals
is almost complete.
There are just two more mammals
I want you to meet.

They are right in this room:
One has brown eyes,
one blue.
These mammals are two of my favorites—
they're...

...you!

Yes, people are mammals—
amazing but true!
Oh, and cats in tall hats?
Well...yes.
We're mammals, too!

GLOSSARY

Breach: To leap from the water.

Carnivore: An animal that eats mostly meat.

Herbivore: An animal that eats mostly plants

Hibernation: A deep state of sleep during the winter.

Mammal: A warm-blooded animal that has a backbone and usually fur or hair and whose babies are fed with milk from their mother's breast.

Omnivore: An animal that eats both meat and plants.

Pygmy: A tiny person, animal, or thing.

Quill: The hollow stem of a feather; the sharp, stiff hair of a porcupine.

INDEX